MW01515710

MY THOUGH

In all I see, I see a world that is corrupted by people; humans.

I see death and destruction
Know death
How death kills
Feel
Smell

I see and know the death of humanity; man
The lies they tell on all including the God they claim to serve; worship.

I see what humans have and has become
I see the wickedness and corruption of them all
The bombs and diseases they create the kill each other; all

Many talk, but behind the facade are people that say they care, but truly don't give a damn.

I see racism
Know racism
The hate of the different races

I see a great divide
Know that divide
Thus I see humans for what they are

Liars and thieves
Haters and spiteful souls and spirits
Rapists and murderers because they do rape you of everything then kill you afterwards.

Some plague your land
Kill you for your land; what truly belong to you

Look at history, the history of man and see what the white man and his race has and have done to the black ones; black race.

They extort and kill us
Take all that belong to us
Turn all in humanity against us

They teach white supremacy
Teach you to hate and loathe your own black skin

They divide mentally and physically including spiritually

They give us their false and dead gods whilst telling us ours is dead when he is truly not dead.

They rape and abuse us
Take away or true peace and dignity

THEY STARVE US OF OUR GOD; BELOVED
THEY'VE DISTANCED HIM FROM US

Now we cannot find him. We've dirtied self; have become filthy and unclean because of the lies they tell us; the brutal beatings they dished out on us to accept them and their false doctrines whilst they rape us of our land and home; riches, culture, language, god and good and clean environment; planet; the planet we call home.

They taught us to wander
Become beggars
Ignorant
Fools that beg them for a bone and so much more

They treat us worse than dogs
Call us animals, but yet they look to a Black God to save them without knowing the god they serve is a Black Man.

All this and more they did and still do to us. If you do not accept them; they eradicate you by any means necessary with their guns and war machines; diseases.

You are forced to give up your truth and life; birthright.
You are forced to bow down to them; praise them.

All this my beloved sees but yet has done nothing in my book to save is true own from the walking, living, breathing, demons and plagues that roam the earth.

He sees the hatred and eradication of another human being by white men that brutalize and kill; thus many in the human race I refuse and truly will not save if I am the saving grace of humanity. I will not save nations that rob and steal willingly and wilfully.

I will not save nations like Germany that have and has done all to eradicate the black man from this planet and universe. Nor will I save any White South African. _**They have done enough wickedness to the Blacks of South Africa thus an eye for an eye and a tooth for a tooth.**_

So as they walk and kill without remorse, I give them no saving grace and will never plea with Lovey for any of them. Life is precious and you've robbed the Black Man enough. Thus I withdraw my truth and goodness from all of you. If Lovey so see it befitting to send someone else to save you, so be it, but I will not save any of you. Thus it is written in this book and I do hope Lovey respects my good heart and will; wishes.

Oh Lovey the evils (Germans and South Africans) have done to my African own wow. But yet we as black people marry them; procreate and forgive them for the atrocities they've done to our black own. They are the true devils in my book. Thus my books; novels that I've written that included them, I must now truly burn because to me they are a curse; vile and wicked; demons that kill at will. They steal; rob you of your self worth. Just look at what they did to Africa and Africans thus no forgiveness in my book for them. They can all go back to hell and rot their indefinitely without end. Don't hate my race and expect the God of Good and True Life to accept you in his kingdom and abode.

Who the hell are you?

You disgrace and mistreat us but yet expect our God to save you. Go figure.

Hence I include no German in your world of truth Lovey. And I truly do not care if there are black Germans; they too are indefinitely locked out of my world and your world for the crimes they have done to our African own despite the way I write in my other books.

How can someone look at another human being and eradicate them just like that?

How can you look at another human being and rob them of everything just like that?

Yes Lovey I know we are to blame because we are the ones to let these demons into our world. Thus immigration is a bitch and burner to some countries until this day.

Look at how White South Africans and Germans degrade and discriminate against Black South Africans and Blacks. Look at the hatred of those Whites towards Blacks and I'm to save them; White South Africans and Germans? I will not do it. I would rather spit on the earth and turn my back on you Lovey rather than save one.

Look at what they did to Nelson Mandela.
27 years they jailed him for for his own right and rights as a human being and he was never vindicated nor was his people vindicated. Now I hope as of this day Lovey you vindicate Black South Africans and let them wake up and live up; rise up in pride and dignity and walk in and on the pathway of righteousness and truth with you. I have hope for them Lovey. I have true hope for them that one day they would put down all violence and crime and live good and free with each other; each one help each other in goodness and in truth in a good and positive way.

Look at the genocide of Germans towards the Nubian and or Namib people, and you want me to have compassion for murderers and thieves that rob Black People of their wealth? Dear God man, how can a....wow, let me leave my brutal comment to myself because you are my true God and God alone. You know my heart and feel because hell is not hot enough for a German as far as I am concerned. Thus the history books of man are a testament and proof to the genocide my people faced. No Lovey, read the history books of man for yourself. And you tell me you are bleeping human. You have no bleeping shame and disgrace; soul because you massacre us; my people and pretend to like us. Some of you marry us and some of us marry you. The feeling of hate should be mutual but I hate you not, I hate you not, I hate you not because I know for a fact hell is there and the lots of you are going to rot there because the debt of your ancestors has not been paid and cannot be paid. So yes, my spirit is rest assured of your hell and rightfully so. So glory to God because I know Britain will pay also. They must pay because you do not rob a man of what rightfully belongs to him. As for you the Portuguese and Spanish, truly woe be unto the lots of you when Hell is done with you.

Truly look Lovey because you have proof of the sins of the fathers and forefathers. Despite our (Black People's) behaviour Lovey, we need to be vindicated. You cannot let the sins of these people and their ancestors go unpunished. ***YOU PUNISHED US BY LEAVING US, SO WHY ARE YOU FORSAKING US WHEN IT COMES TO THESE WICKED AND EVIL PEOPLE?***

Did you not allow them to colonize us and rob us of you? Did you not allow the brutality of the Black Race globally and not one tear did you shed for us?

Look at the brutality I faced in my life and not one tear you shed for me and say no, you cannot do this to her?

How much more should have to suffer Lovey before you come to your knees in tears and say no more, this isn't fair, the vileness of humanity; humans to humans and humans to earth must stop and stop now? How long must you go on seeing the sufferings; vile murders here on earth and do nothing about it?

Look at how blacks are being discriminated against globally. And you want me to save the white race?

Did you not show me them as being cursed? *She the White Woman of old cursed them because all they do is fight and kill; rape you of your wealth and dignity and nothing has changed with them until this day. So why should I save any?*

I will not save any and you cannot make me save them because in truth ***THEY ARE TRULY NOT OUR PEOPLE.*** And this has nothing to do with hue Lovey; it has all to do with wicked and evil deeds. ***THUS WHITE DEATH AND BLACK DEATH LIVE WITH MAN, TALK TO MAN AND WALK WITH MAN; HUMANS EACH AND EVERY DAY.***

How can anyone look at another race and eradicate them like that without thought and care? Thus I tell you everyone need a mother and father and you refuse to listen to me.

You left us Lovey due to the evils that we do, but you cannot abandon our good and true people. We need you, so truly return to us. It's not fair for the wicked and evil of this and outer world to continually take us to hell with them.

It's not fair for anyone to rob us of you come on now. You are our right and you are not listening to me. When do you begin to hear Lovey?

Why should our ties be severed with you come on now?

You cannot say you love us so and leave us to die and I've told you this.

You cannot say you've given me seeds to plant over one hundred million acres and not tell me how to plant these seeds.

Where's the tools to till the land?

Where is the clean water to grow these seeds?

Where is the sunlight to shine on these seeds to help them grow?

Where is the good and clean; pure and honest earth to plant these seeds in so that they can grow good and clean; pure and wholesome that is void of chemicals, insects and sin?

Are these seeds that you've given me not good?

I need them good and true not ugly and filled with sin and all manner of wickedness and sin.

Lovey if you are not whole and good, none of us can be whole and good come on now. You cannot continue to kill us by leaving your doors closed to us come on now. We want to come home and you're not letting us.

Tell me something, what is the point of me being true to you and you are not true to me?

Can a daughter and or car run on one cylinder?

Lovey, if your cylinder is broken, can I drive you or even come to you for help and or a lift; ride?

If your engine is failing, will your car not eventually die?

If your transmission is broken can your car drive?

SO NOW TELL ME THIS LOVEY, HOW CAN WE AS HUMANS DO WITHOUT YOU?

ARE WE NOT BROKEN AND CANNOT BE FIXED BECAUSE YOU'VE LEFT US TO DIE DUE TO OUR WICKEDNESS AND SINS?

Are we not failing you due to sins and hate?

Go back to the above and how Germany tried to eradicate all the black people in Namib; Namibia. Yes Namib is protected by you because the desert made sure it fought against the Germans and won against man in their own special way. No it could not stop the mass killings but it made sure it protects Nubia; Namib until this day. Peace; true peace and blessings Nubia, true peace and happiness because you are protected by the Most High God; Lovey until this day. Continue to walk in true peace. And may true peace continue to strive in you always and forever because you more than deserve it. May Lovey continue to protect and guard all of you because one day your ancestors will be vindicated for the atrocities done to them by foreign invaders.

So Lovey, no white people can tell me nothing. THEY WERE BORN IN INIQUITY AND SHAPED IN DEATH. THUS THEY LIVE TO KILL AND THEY DO KILL ALL EVERYWHERE THEY GO AND THAT IS A CRYING SHAME.

Yes the undertone cannot be helped Lovey because I do not base anything on hue. THUS YOU MUST DO A BETTER JOB IN SEPARATING THE TRUE AND GOOD WHITE PEOPLE THAT FALL UNDER YOUR GOOD AND TRUE BLACK BANNER FROM THE REST OF THE WICKED; WICKED WORLD.

Just as how you have separated your good and true black people that fall under your good and true black banner from the rest of the wicked; wicked world, separate your true white own also.

We need this Lovey.
We can no longer cohabited and or live with the wicked and evil of this world.

So yes, without a shadow of a doubt and with all my true and unconditional love and true heart, YES, I WANT TO GO TO NAMIBIA AND SEE FOR MY SELF.

I NEED TO SEE THE ANCIENTS OF THIS LAND.

I NEED TO TALK TO HIM AND YES THEM; THE PEOPLE OF THE LAND.

LOVEY, IF IT BE THY WILL, LET THIS TRAVEL BE IN 2016 BECAUSE I NEED TO KNOW SOMETHING. I TRULY BELIEVE AND KNOW TO MYSELF THAT WHAT I SEEK IS TRULY THERE.

Yes I have to go to Mongolia and Siberia, Russia but Namib is truly where I need and want to be right now.

I need to be there Lovey, so truly take me there in goodness and in truth. I need to write about what I see there. So truly make a good and positive, clean and honest including positive and good financial way for me to go there; get there.

Lovey let not my health hinder me from traveling there. Remember the black lady in my dream that told me if she could help me with my sickness she would. I know she could not help me because my true help does not come from her, it comes from you. So truly help me to go to Namibia as of January 2016.

I need you not in death Lovey but in true life.

The world is changing thus I know the harvest that is coming and the starvation that will be upon land globally.

I know lands are sinking and is going to sink into the seas and oceans but that's okay by me. Humans are the ones to create this mess due to greed and global warming.

We (me and you) Lovey need to replenish the land and lands of earth. But we need to do it positive and clean so that no human being or spirit can come and destroy what we've rebuild.

We need to be free Lovey and I have to roam and roll with you positively.

I have to roam and roll with you clean and true.

So stop this abandonment business. Let the wicked and evil go because they mean you no good and you know this.

Stop the hindrance of me by wicked and evil spirits and people. I truly don't need it anymore because I've found where I truly need to be.

I see peace; true peace and I more than truly need it. I need you but you are not listening. You need to stop hiding from me and let us truly go home; find our good and true home here on earth.

I know Cayman is for you, but in truth Namib is truly for me. I want and need to see the desert up close and personal, and yes I want to kiss it; kiss the desert and say truly thank you for your gift of life. Wow Lovey I know, I know the truth and see the truth; truly thank you Lovey.

Lovey you know the life I see so yes I truly want and need to go to Namib and you are going to truly help me. Yes I am bullying you and I am sorry, but Lovey I truly want and need to go. Think Moses and the Red Sea Lovey, think Moses and the Red Sea. Wow

So can we, can we, can we. I am so excited Lovey. Please open up Namib; Namibia to me and you in a good and true way.

Thank you Lovey.

Truly thank you, thank you, thank you.

Michelle
October 10 & 15, 2015

Wow Lovey. I am so going to stop trying to decipher my dreams because I so decipher wrong.

Death you are a bitch nigger when it comes to death.

Humanity is a bitch as well when it comes to certain nasty shit that they do.

When a man truly don't like you they will pretend to like you and give you basket with holes to carry water. Thus life it truly not valued by all.

Therefore my dream with the dead baby came through. The dead child was my daughter's friend first child. Thus the ugly fishes represented the agony that poor child was going through in the mother's womb. Therefore I know the nastiness that some human's do to take and or snatch a life from another human being.

Oh Namibia, Namibia I want to come home
I want to live in you
Roam free
Be me
Free

Oh Namibia you are enchanting
Ancient
A beautiful queen

I need to dream of you

See all that is in you to see
I need to fly around in you
Walk
Talk
Do all the good I need to do

Oh Namibia, Namibia I am truly missing you even though I truly do not know you.

Namibia, do you dream of me?
Know me?
Do you even want to find me?
Roam good and free with me?

Oh Namibia, Namibia can you truly love me?

Can we be wild together by walking barefoot in the sand?
Can I plant yams, corn, bamboo, mango trees in you?

Yes breadfruit and cactus will do too.
Will the sand mind if I blessed them truly with trees of green?

Ah Namibia, Namibia I am calling out to you. Will you answer me and truly receive me?

Michelle and Michelle Jean

Yes it's early morning October 11th 2015 and I so cannot go back to sleep. Forgot to put in one of my books that I dreamt the condemnation of Chris Brown. I can't remember what he did if he was arguing. All I know is that he was condemned. Oh well such is life because I've been seeing and or telling people they are condemned.

Listen people our choice and or choices including negative actions can and will get us condemned so that we cannot enter the realm and world of Lovey.

Oh man I can't remember if I was on a planet and fighting broke out. As of late space flights and fighting are being kept from me. So I have to watch this dream to see if there is going to be another mass killing in the United States or somewhere globally, but particular the United States. It seems when I see these dreams it's there someone target in the school system and or somewhere else. I am so not going to elaborate because these space fights are uncharted territory to me; meaning they are truly not straight when it comes to the targeted territory of death. Death mask death for me hence I will do my best not to decipher my dreams anymore.

Also, earlier in the morning I had this weird waking state vision of the sea. It's like a space was outlined for me with squiggly lines and the sea and or time and or the earth was spinning counter clockwise. There was a huge sink hole in the sea with water being drained into it. I am going to see if I can find the lines on Google, the circle and or rotation of the counter clockwise spin and the sink hole I am talking about for you to see. Yes I so did not want to put dreams in this book but I guess I have to. The sea dream waking state vision is stuck in my head and I cannot let it go until I write about it it seems.

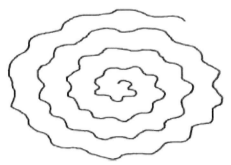

This is the best picture I can find that describes the circular squiggly line I am talking about. There was only one line but you get the drift. I don't know why the African Tectonic Plate is stuck in my head, but you can use this plate as an example of size but bigger. ***If you combine the African Plate and the South American Plates and add some of the Caribbean Plate you will get the size and or mass of the circle with the squiggly line that I am talking about.***

So far nothing with the counter clockwise rotation and or motion on Google, but will keep searching. Nothing under crop circle that remotely fit the description of the rotation of the circle I saw within the squiggly line. No for Stonehenge which is Pi. Oh man this is proving difficult for me, so I am going back to crop circle. There is a picture there I can use but the picture have to be dissected. Now I can't find the image darn it but will keep searching.

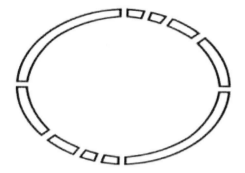

This is not the best picture but you see the two large rectangular like circle. This is the picture of the rotation. Now think of the rectangle standing up from an aerial standpoint; as in Stonehenge kinda like standing up. Oh man I hope I have not confused you but hope you get the drift of what I am trying to show you.

This is a better picture of what I am talking about. See the barges outside this sea port. It's something like this but without the circles at the end and more upright. And no do not use the Belize Blue Hole Picture because it isn't it.

As for the deep hole in the sea, here we go because there is many to choose from and anyone will do except the water must be blue. It was blue waters I saw and not red or clear. This picture represents the hole I am talking about but without the mountain or hill in the back drop.

And as usual, all pictures used in this book are for the sole purpose of illustration only. They are to show you and or guide you in what I see, so that you will know and figure things out. Waking state visions or dreams I cannot figure out, thus I put no value to them because I truly do not know what they mean. If you do great, but I don't. Maybe this vision is for scientists to look into things who knows.

Further I cannot tell you the region I saw this vision in but the India Bangladesh and Indonesia regions come to mind. Please do not quote me on these regions. Like I said, I did not see the region in my vision thus I cannot tell you which region this vision represent.

I truly do not know if all of Oceania is going to sink. I know something big is looming and for me to see the size of it is crazy despite me not putting value on waking visions or dreams. I know it's crazy and I so do not want to send anyone on a wild goose chase, but the sea is going to take back her land and lands from humans. ***Thus I've told you long ago in another book that NOAH'S ARK IS HERE. THE TIME OF NOAH IS NOW AND WAS NOT THEN.***

Billions are going to lose their lives because of our greed, selfishness and wickedness towards each other.

We created this hell with our sins. Now the true black race must find home and leave out of Babylon globally.

Lovey cannot save the devil's own. He must truly leave them alone because in all humans do here on earth; we do not know nor do we see that our sins do affect earth.

We only think of self. We do not truly think of the planet we live in.

We do not secure Mother Earth, so Mother Earth can no longer secure us. She must give us over to the hell and or hells we created for self. Earth is a part of good and true life but she can no longer sustain us because we've polluted her beyond repair. It's going to take thousands of centuries for her to begin to heal due to the damage of man; us as humans.

Earth is sick; dying and we as humans are the cause of her death. We created the mess in her and instead of fixing her little by little, we continue to add more pollutants; chemical and garbage in her. ***WE'VE FORGOTTEN THE MOTTO, GARBAGE IN, GARBAGE OUT.*** So if we put all our garbage in Mother Earth, we are going to get back garbage and this is what's happening to humanity today with the food we eat and the water we drink.

We talk about sustainability but we cannot sustain ourselves. We truly do not think of the future nor do we think of future generations. We put value on self whilst raping earth of her resources. We do not give her good food to eat to maintain her nor do we maintain her waterways.

We take all now and build monuments to say, look, my land is better because I've built bigger than you. I reach further into the sky without knowing that what goes up, must eventually come down. All you build and show off on must be left barren and empty.

The fall of humans is here.

Humans are going to fall; thus the God and Gods you seek will be nowhere in sight because they've all left man.

And truly don't go there because there is only one God and that God is Lovey.

Different races have their god and gods thus Lovey accepts them not, nor does he see these people. He Lovey cannot. Therefore, when we sin and or continuously do wrong, he leaves us to our own demise and rightfully so.

*Oh man did I stray from this book. So let's get right into what I wrote on paper. THUS HUMANITY, **I GIVE YOU AND DEDICATE REAL SITUATION BY BOB MARLEY (ROBERT NESTA MARLEY) TO ALL OF YOU.** He did tell you but you did not want to hear; listen. He did tell you, **"total destruction is the only solution and there isn't any use, no one can stop them now."** So truly good luck to all of you because **DESTRUCTION COMETH AND NO ONE ON THE FACE OF THIS PLANET CAN STOP IT BECAUSE DESTRUCTION WAS ORDAINED DUE TO OUR CONTINUAL SIN AND SINS; WICKEDNESS.***

*Humans globally have and has amassed a debt load with death that no one can repay. Hence we were told, **"THE WAGES OF SIN IS DEATH."***

Michelle Jean

Now Lovey I have to wonder about you.
I have to wonder if you truly care about me.
Do you truly care about anyone or anything Lovey?

Look at the trials and tribulations in this world.
Look at the earth on a whole.

For someone who say you love us so, I have to doubt you.
How can your loving us so leave us broken and abandoned?

How can you love us so and watch earth being deteriorated like this?

What wrong did the earth do to you for you to forsake her so?

Lovey is loving us so war and lies to you for us?

Is loving us so, your dark truth; denial?

What does loving us so mean to you?
Are you not heavenly; spiritual and physical?

So if you are all these things Lovey, why are you not true?

Why keep us running around in a circle of mazes trying to find you?

Why let evil cage us in?
You want us to listen to you but do you truly listen to us?

Do you truly care about us?

Michelle and Michelle Jean
September 28, 2015

Hope fades
Lives lost
Lies told
Death toll rises; fades
Then rise again

Sanity comes
Sanity goes
The maze and mazes of life
You walk from home
Go home

Work only to go to work again.
Oh what sense do I make? I cannot comprehend loving so on this day.

How can you say you love us so Lovey and see so much confusion here on earth and do nothing about it?

All that we've been taught is based on lies but yet humans kill to keep these lies. Lies are readily accepted over the truth. Judicial systems here on earth were created to protect the guilty – liars. Man swear on their so called holy book to tell the truth but yet tell lies to protect self.

So tell me Lovey, how can you love us so when the system (s) of men were created to keep us sinning; keep us away from you?

You see and know this but yet in all that you do, you cannot fix the lies of man. You let the lies continue and that's truly a shame.

Michelle and Michelle Jean
September 28, 2015

So what good is loving us so?
What purpose does loving us so serve?

In all of your loving us so Lovey, did you think of the earth; Mother Earth, Nature and or the environment?

Do you love them (the earth), nature and or the environment so also?

D you truly care?
Why punish them because of man; humans?

Did the environment and waterways sin against you too?
What vile act did nature commit against you?

So why punish them for the sins of man; humans by continuing to let humans destroy them?

Yes I know the sinking and separation of lands.
I know my truth to you and it still stands.

But Lovey, what did nature; the waterways; this earth do to you for you to hate them so?

Why abandon them?
Why leave them unprotected?

Yes the questions are many Lovey but I have to do this. I need to get out of my environment but it seems I am stuck here.

I need to be free but yet you won't let me leave. You keep me in prison against my will.

This land is my hell here on earth. I can't take it anymore; hence I am caged; burdened and bogged down. My spirit is not free hence the spirit is caged in this hell; prison that we call flesh; home.

Michelle and Michelle Jean
September 28, 2015

How I loathe hell; this prison that keeps my spirit captive. How I loathe this land that I am being kept in.

No good will do I have for this land on this day. I want out but Lovey won't let me.

How can a god say they love you so but yet keep you shackled and chained in hell?

My body is dirty and my spirit want to flee it at will.

What grave injustice is this Lovey?
Why keep us from you?

Why chain us and leave us in a dirty and filthy body?

Tell me, how fair are you?

Why lie to me and keep me in hell?

No one can thoroughly clean their body Lovey you know this. So why walk away from us if our body cannot become fully clean; whole?

Can a man or woman including child become clean if their surroundings is constantly dirty; unclean?

Tell me something. If we are conditioned to accept lies and tell lies, will we not become liars and thieves?

So how can you as Good God and Allelujah, Lovey justify your loving us so?

You are clean but yet you love unclean so?

By YOU loving us so, does that not make you dirty also?

Are you not telling me, you love dirty and unclean? Hence the ugly man did tell me you answer him right away.

So what good is truly loving you unconditionally ***when you too are dirty and you keep us dirty; unclean?***

Michelle and Michelle Jean
September 28, 2015

It's October 15$^{th, 2015}$ and I am so going to interrupt the flow of this book again. Fam and People Lovey is or can be a bitch nigga when he wants to be.

I was so excited to go to Namibia and guess what; he burst my bubble big time this morning. Africa and or at least Namibia is off my radar, I cannot go there. Remember how I wanted to go to Blue Mountain, Collingwood and he Lovey refused me entry by drying up the trees and I went ballistic on him in another book. Well this is the same with Namibia but it was not the trees of this land that dried up.

Fam and People, if I go to Namibia, I will be tied up and confused.

I would be wandering in a bed and or sea of confusion. I

know this is not the first time Lovey has shown me this confusion, so I am going to leave Africa alone for now. It's funny though. I want to go to Russia, Siberia and Mongolia and he does not object, but yet object to me going to Africa for a while. Go figure. Listen Fam and People, if I go to Namibia the sea will dry up and become desert and I truly do not want or need this to happen to Mama Africa; so I will abide by Lovey's decision. And yes, I actually saw the sea drying up with the confusion in my dream earlier this morning. Trust me, I got up to go the bathroom and kept getting tangled in my clothes. My dream world or state would not stop in regards to my confusing state if I went to Namibia; thus I was tangled up in my clothes. So this country I have to truly leave alone. Yes I know why.

Think the Mountain of Lovey and the section of the mountain that I chose. Once you've made a decision with Lovey, you have to stick to that decision come what may. So know that certain lands Lovey do forbid you to go into. I know what Mama Africa did Lovey. But is all of Africa forbidden to me? Do tell because I truly want and need to know. Kenya I know I can go to from your standpoint, but why not Namibia?

How about Zambia and Angola?

Seychelles I know you have no objections to because I want to go there and you've not objected, but yet Namibia you object to me going. Is it the kissing of the desert that I want to do? Or is it the <u>VALLEY OF THE DEAD THAT I WANT TO GO INTO?</u> Truly tell because you are ONE JEALOUS GOD. This I truly know now, but still your jealousy is not as deep as mine.

I also dreamt Buju Banton (Mark Myrie) again. Beenie Man was in the dream and I asked him if he knew what the crossed sword that they put on Buju meant and he said yes. I believe he said he was going to check out something and let me know and or he was going to watch and see. I can't remember his exact words people. But from the dream, **_and in my opinion,_** I gather it was someone in the music industry that crossed this man with a sword. Thus Obeah nuh stop inna Jamaica.

I cannot tell you who crossed Buju but when I find out I will let you know who the culprit is.

I am going to ask the question and truly do not take it the wrong way, but Beenie Man a yu cross di man? Mi affi ask because sey anno di first time me a dream si yu inna Buju vision or dream. Soh mi ask again, a yu cross di man with di sword? Only time will tell people because time do tell no matter how long it takes. Thus the vile and wickedness of my Jamaican own never stop because Obeah chat, chop, an walk; an Obeah do catch their intended target no matter what. **_Therefore, as good and true people, you have to guard yourself from the wicked and evil of society._**

Further, for those of you who follow dreams and live by them, know that dreams repeat cycles. Meaning some dreams do circle and come around again. So dreams do repeat itself. **ONWARDS I GO.**

Michelle and Michelle Jean

Why do I feel hopeless when I think of you Lovey?
Why do I feel as if you are all a game?
Why do I feel set up by you; lost; confused?

I am thinking Lovey and if you loving us so is so great, why are we dazed and confused; in such disarray?

Why leave us behind if you love us so?

Why keep us prisoners in lands and homes that are not ours?

Why leave us conquered and abused; without a true home?

You know what the Babylonians did to us, but yet we still praise and worship their god and gods. **_Are you Babylonian Lovey and is this why you do nothing to truly help your true own?_**

Egypt became nasty thus sexual perversion was rampant. I know because I see; saw and heard the voices in my head.

Oh man Nefertiti. We as blacks praise her, say she's black but she was not black; she was Babylonian; Hindu. Thus I heard the voices and Babylonian music in my head. The dead made sure I heard this.

Wow she was a nasty whore; loved sexual perversion; was the mother of them all.

Oh well, such is life I guess when you are of a different realm and world.

Many things black people; the true black race do not know thus they do not keep in contact with their true spiritual side. They cannot see the dead walk nor can they hear them talk and this is truly a crying shame. Evil can be stopped, but who is ordained to stop evil in this day and time when evil is more than universal and global?

We do not connect with our spirit in order to know the truth.

Thus the White and Black generation will be forever lost because they forgot they were and still are a true family.

It is sad that it is only when the pitting and hatred stop we will know the full and true truth.

Michelle and Michelle Jean
September 29, 2015
Edited October 15, 2015

It's 2:53 in the morning Lovey and I have to interrupt this book because I cannot go back to sleep. And forgive me if I come across as rude and bold face. ***But what is the difference between you and a human male?***

No, truly tell me because my thoughts are different on this day and I truly have to ask.

You told me on more than one occasion if I leave you; disobey you; I will not be able to find you. But if we do not have true direction are we not lost?

Are you not gone from us already so are you not lost to us? So now tell me, how can I find what I truly do not have?

Look at how many fathers globally that have abandoned their responsibility as a father and mother. Have you not done the same thing?

<u>No, I cannot forget about our sins but Lovey, if you were a true father and family man from the get go, would we be this way today?</u>

Have you not left and gone to other people seeking acceptance?

Have other gods not come into the picture where man; humans worship trees and animals?

So tell me, what have you done as a true father to heal the pain and sufferings of our good and true people?

You see our needs and instead of truly helping you run away. If you don't run, it takes decades for some, years for others, days, months and weeks for some to get a tat of help from you. You see our ailments but instead of giving us the right treatment to heal and fix our self you leave us broken; in ruin.

So what is the difference between you and a man; human especially a sinful and greedy human?

I use to be greedy for you but not anymore. Well not to the extent that I use to. I cannot comprehend the scope of you building and humans just come along and breakdown; destroy just like that. So why build faulty in the first place?

Why build at all?

So then if you build faulty; are we not damaged goods?

If the father is faulty then the children will become faulty also. Thus you are confusion all around.

You are no different from a man, because man; humans do not build to last; they build to destroy. Nothing about you and this world is true Lovey. Look around globally, men rule with an iron fist. They are corrupt and greedy.

Men desire power and control and if they cannot get it, they kill and destroy for it. Let's go back to Germans and what they have done to Blacks and Whites. Now tell me, **_were these men sane?_**

Power and control makes people ruthless and evil. They have power, so they've lost their minds because they take freedom from their people and the society they live in come on now. Do they not know how much people hate and loathe them?

No, they cannot see the evils that they are doing because these vile and disgusting men think they are doing nothing wrong. They have power and control thus they can do anything to their people and this is truly a crying shame. You want to rule but yet you deny your people the basic necessities of life and think you are doing good. Bitch Nigga you're not good. You are evil and you are a disgrace to humanity. Thus you take your land and people to hell with you to burn. Good does not take the right and rights away from their people. Good does not take their people's freedom from them come on now. **_So if you were good, why do YOU ABUSE YOUR PEOPLE?_**

So tell me Lovey, are you truly any different from man?

Yes I know you are the protector, but how well do you protect if evil; wicked and evil people and spirits can infiltrate and hurt your own people?

Now look at the course of history and see who were the vile and evil ones in all of this. ***HAVE MEN NOT BEEN DECEIVING FROM THE BEGINNING OF TIME?***

So what makes you any different from a man?

Yes I know you are female also but truly Lovey; look into yourself and see the destructive nature of man; humans.

Now tell me, if you had built clean and valued cleanliness of all, would the earth be so filthy with the sins of man; humans?

Would it?

If you had valued earth, and was true to Mother Earth, would you have set humans to walk on land and destroy her?

So tell me, what wrong did Mother Earth do you that you had to set and or create and or form humans in her to destroy her?

I will ask again, what hatred do you have for her Mother Earth that you would allow humans to destroy her like that and or this?

So in all that I know and see, when it comes to your good and true females as a father you value and cherish us not.

So tell me now, if this is the case, why should we value you and do all to obey you?

If mother and father care not for a child, why should a child grow to truly love and care for that mother or father?

Isn't that child condemning self and allowing crap and or shit to happen to him or her?

Goodness and truth value goodness and truth.

I feed off and strive for goodness and truth, but you truly don't. Thus why should any human walk with you when you truly do not know how to walk with them?

How can you value cleanliness when you too are truly not clean in my book?

If I am clean and a dirty person come into my domain; isn't my domain not dirty? So how can you look to anyone of us for cleanliness when our surroundings are dirty; unclean?

Yes I've asked you this and you've not answered me. So truly don't tell me you love us so when you truly do not.

Absolutely no one can live on "LOVE US SO." I certainly can't. So why taint yourself and expect us to still be clean?

Why tell me about loving so when loving so in my book is truly not clean?

Why Lovey?

Why?

Can clean create unclean?

No, come on tell me. Can clean create unclean?

So why do you allow humans to believe you are unclean?
Why do allow me to question you in this way?
Am I missing the bigger picture with you?

I see death
I see the birth of life
I see and know pain. But with all this said; where are you truly?

Where's the true comfort in you when all we on earth know and see is evil? We see it and live in it. So is earth our true heaven and hell; bombs of life?

Are we not living in hell here?
Do we not destroy everything hence the two H's?

So if this is the case Lovey, how can we truly find you in chaos; an unclean world?

Michelle Jean
October 12 and 15, 2015

Yes it's weird Lovey because these are my thoughts.
I truly have to think and come to you in this way.

It's weird how I have so many questions and you are not answering them all.

It's as if you fail to see the big picture in all of this.

No our relationship is not fragile. But you truly have to do better when it comes to me and our good and true people.

Lovey, what is the defining moment in your life?

You have male and female and one is more destructive and deadlier than the other. Why?

Why are men so destructive and wicked; evil?

Why do they have to kill and destroy to get what they want?

Lovey going back to her when she said, "God kills," how do you react to this?

What made her tell me this?

What made the ugly black man tell me you answer him right away?

Do I over value you Lovey?

DO I VALUE YOU SO MUCH THAT I PUT YOU SO HIGH THAT I FAIL TO SEE AND KNOW THE REAL AND TRUE YOU?

Right now I truly don't know Lovey because I truly cannot over stand or comprehend why you would value evil over good.

Now tell me, how can I recommend you when I am truly not sure of you and your loyalty to our good and true people sometimes?

How can I say you are true to good and true life when all I see around me is dishonour and death; the selfishness and greed of humanity?

Now tell me Lovey, are you selfish and greedy like men; humans?

Have you destroyed it all to gain it all in a negative way?

Now tell me, why do you destroy us as females?

Why do you take all from us and let men abuse us; a lot of us in the living?

Why allow men to use and degrade women?

If you are the true female in us, <u>why do you truly not care?</u>

Why do you not desire good and true life?

If you were truly female Lovey, **<u>why let men destroy this planet; planet earth?</u>**

If you were truly a mother, the female in me, <u>why are you truly not nurturing?</u>

So why lie to me, when you have no true and good female traits?

I've told you about true love but you have no true love in you in my book and yes on this day. **<u>If you truly loved, would you let people destroy all that you created; gave birth to?</u>**

So how can you truly be female when I cannot see the female in you on this day? Yes these are my thoughts; hence I have to get them out no matter how negative they sound. Lovey no one can walk on one foot. We need both legs because each one help the other; are balanced. So why do you leave us to walk on one foot? *And people I know some people can walk on one foot because I've seen it in a video. A one legged bicycle courier in Nairobi, Kenya.*

Maybe it's me you leave to walk on one foot with these books. And in truth you do because I have no true help from males in the spiritual realm, thus I am so left alone. I am going back to bed and leaving you alone for now. My world and your world are not the same; nor are they on the same level Lovey.

You continue to let the wicked and evil dominate.
You continue to let the wicked and evil kill.

But what about the good in this world?
What about the earth itself?

Why leave us to be brutalized beyond repair Lovey? Look at how many children that need their father and do not have them in their lives to guide them. Do you not do the same thing?

I told you I wanted to go to Namibia and you said no in your way. But in saying no, you did not tell me the reason why you do not want me to go. I have to figure it out for myself. ***THUS I TELL YOU TIME AND TIME AGAIN THAT YOU ARE A LOUSY TEACHER BUT A GREAT PROTECTOR.*** You cannot protect without teaching Lovey. I know certain things we are not to do and I truly hope that I've taught my readers well in these books. Yes I know some things are truly hard to explain but I do my best. What I cannot explain in writing I am hoping drawings and or pictures help me to convey the messages you want and need me to deliver.

We know religion kills.
We know politics kills.

We know about physical and spiritual death.
We know about life and death.
We know about hue; colour of skin and or flesh.
We know how our sins look.
We know what the rich man's sins look like.
We know who are condemned in life thus there is no saving grace for them when the spirit leaves the flesh.

We know what automatic deaths are.
We know what the fire of hell look like.
We know what Satan look like.

We know what Black and White Death look like.
We know what Female Death look like.

All this and more we know because I've tried my best to educate humanity on these things and or them in these books. I tell them and try to show them what I see as given to me by you. So humanity cannot say they don't know because knowledge was given unto them in these books.

Michelle and Michelle Jean
October 12 and 15, 2015

Wow because I did sleep and it's one thing about you Lovey is that you don't like to be questioned in certain way. Thus my questioning this morning unnerved you but in truth I truly don't care.

In a nut shell you are telling me to pick the beam out of my eye before I pick it out of yours thus you showed me my kitchen with yellow ooze oozing out of it and you showed me him moving my stove; all the heavy stuff in my kitchen and almost dropping down. I could see the sweat running off his body. *__He's still thin thus he's clinging to me because he's trying to avoid prison; hell. But like I've told you, I will not save him. I refuse to because of the evil and wickedness he's done to me in the living.__* *I did not hurt him but did all to help him. Instead of cherishing goodness and keeping goodness safe, he did all to destroy and kill me in the living as well as in death.* I will not take back my words to you Lovey. So no matter how you bring him up, I refuse more than unconditionally and truthfully to save him. You do not destroy goodness for your own evil schemes and plots. Thus I've told you time and time again; if I am the saving grace for humanity, I will not save anyone or anything including spirits who are and or that is wicked and evil. I refuse to and you and my truth and more than unconditional true love of you and all that is good and true cannot make me do this. I would rather disobey you than save them and you have my word of truth on this. You also know this because evil know the evils they have done. They (evil) wilfully sin and is expecting someone to save them including die for them and this cannot work Lovey. Good should never have to suffer for evil and wicked people.

You allow wicked and evil people to control, dominate and destroy. Look at the history books of man including the videos and pictures on the internet of man. You will see and know the evils that the white and black race; all races have and has done. I don't have to write them in these books. You have more than historical facts of these wickedness, so truly don't show me him and think I am going to fall into your trap. I know my home is dirty and need a thorough cleaning. So truly don't go there with him and him moving my stove. I do the best I can when I can due to illness. I know the hell he's in and no matter how he moves my stove to show me this as well, I will not save him. Let him rot and burn in hell because he did all to take me away from you. He made me curse you amongst others things and I will never forgive him for this. He broke me down. He did all to kill me and you know this Lovey, so truly do not go there with him because I did face more than hell with him in my life and in his death come on now. You know the truth but yet you flaunt it at me. So yes turnabout is fair play in your book. It's now word for word when it comes to me and you. Touché, you got me Lovey, you truly got me.

Also for you to be showing me me atop a mountain lined with men and women at the edge repeating some of the things I've written is so not fair on your part. So truly be angry because I know this is your way of saying you are angry at me for what I wrote. And like I said, I truly do not care if you are angry or upset at me. I have to repeat myself over and over with you because you truly do not get it when it comes to me. I told you in another book that I need you to think and you are truly not doing it. You are the one prolonging the inevitable and this need to stop.

I've told you in another book, well the one prior to this that you are the one on the sidelines jumping up and down saying pick me pick me and no one is picking you.

What do you not get when it comes to humans?

We cannot see you.

Earth is in a mess due to us and by you leaving us do not help anyone. Yes I know we created the mess but none has learned that you will not help us fix it. **_Meaning you are not going to come into a dirty planet and be our Molly Maid and clean up after us._** *We created and or made the mess, and we as humans must clean up after self and fix the messes and mess of this world; that which we created.*

Humans did not choose you.

We left you alone and made death the choice of all. We did sin and allow death to come into our lives and yes this planet and destroy us. So yes we are to blame.

Remember the saying one bad apple spoil di ole bunch.

Well di one bad apple did spoil all of earth. That one bad apple caused the destruction of man and earth; the home you put us in to live. Now man seek other planets to go and call home so that they can spread evil and destroy the home and homes of other life forms and you are allowing this to happen; thus space exploration.

So tell me, what good have you done towards your creation, if you as God and Lovey can make man; humans destroy all.

You are showing me that you are weak and I've told you in another book that I do not want or need a weak God. *Humans should not have to destroy all that you've created and spread evil anywhere, but you allow this to happen.*

So how can you say you are God when man; humans destroy you and all you've created day by day?

So now you are angry at me for asking you what makes you different from man?

You should not be angry because like I said, men are the vile and evil ones. They seek dominance and control; power, and if they cannot have it they will destroy and kill you and this is what's happened over the centuries. Men wage war and kill you for your territory and the white race in hue just to bring hue into this have and has done this. Above I've told you what the Germans did to Africans in Africa and their white counterparts in their land and other places.

White people in hue just to bring hue into this because this is truly my thoughts and freedom with you Lovey has and have plagued the earth with their sickness; disease and massacring of other races; people especially the black race on a whole.

They seek power and control when all your good and true people ever want it true peace and harmony; balance; true balance with you and nature, the universe and our surroundings. We do not seek to kill nor do we seek to war with anyone and you know this. You cannot deny these facts, thus I sympathize with no one that is wicked and evil because they know the evils and wickedness they have done. I truly love you and I have to be totally honest and true with you and to you. Yes you do not like me comparing you to man; humans but guess what, I truly thank you for pointing out my flaws and telling me that my home is dirty and that you have feelings; you do hurt from some of my words. I will not get upset at you for this because time and time again you show me the mess in my home. I cannot move the fridge or stove but guess what; my son did not do a good job in mopping the floors yesterday so I am going to have to redo it. So thank you and one day by my grace and mercy; the goodness I have for me, you, my family and the good and true seeds you've given me, I will be out of a dirty home and land and into a clean one where I can wash myself and keep myself clean for everyone. So truly don't go there. No, yes you can. Thus I ask you this, if you know my home is dirty and I keep complaining to you about my home and the mess in it, why do you keep me in it?

Should you not help me to come out of it in a good and true way?

You see my struggles of getting out and instead of helping me to rise up out of it, you keep me stranded and abandoned in the mess you are complaining about. *We both complain about the same thing but yet you are doing absolutely nothing to help me come out of it. Go figure Lovey come on now. Thus maybe I put you too much on high and give you too much of my truth too much.*

Let me ask you this Lovey; don't hold your head down because you know what I am going to ask you. ***Do you put me on high Lovey?***

You can't truly love because you can only love so. So what is the point of me giving you my good up good up more than unconditional love of truth and you cannot do the same for me? What's the point of me doing this Lovey and you see the hindrance in my life and can't help me break these hindrance walls down in the physical and spiritual realm down?

So now I ask, is this your loving so?

And once again, is your loving so keeping us shackled and chained in hell; land and lands that we do not want to reside and die in; be in?

I talk about you being fair and just, but in all I see and know, I know the unjust and unfair you. Thus humans do not choose you for life; they truly take their chances with death. Death gives them what they need.

But death is not life you say.

But death is life for billions because death is all they see and know and not life. *This is the reality of it all Lovey, and you have to accept this reality.* You allowed sin and or death 24000 to destroy humanity and this has and have happened because humanity is slated to die globally before 2032. This I cannot and will not change because as humans we brought death upon our self. *THIS IS OUR **REAL SITUATION;** ROBERT NESTA MARLEY (BOB MARLEY).*

We did not choose right and for me to say Lovey, you cannot let all of humanity die I would be wrong. Like I said, billions did not choose you, they chose death and death must take them globally. This was the decision of man; humans globally. If we had wanted life, we would have chosen good and true life and that is you. So you cannot cling to humanity; all in humanity because ALL in humanity truly do not belong to you. You have to let death's children go because it's over. Death lost so you have to let them go.

So despite the way I am with you, I have to come to you true. You know what Lovey, it's a pity you were not and or not cut from my true, pure, overly clean and wonderful, truly devoted and righteous, good; truly good cloth that surrounds my pure and good heart; world. Maybe if you were, you would know what true love is all about and yes, you would know what true peace is all about and strive for this true peace all day long and all year round.

No, I am not above you because I truly cannot be you. I have to be truly me; the true me, thus we are truly different in so many ways.

Do you enjoy LIFE Lovey?
Do you truly enjoy life?

Now tell me, what was the point of creating it all when man; humans destroy it all?

Michelle
October 12 and 15, 2015

So in all that I do Lovey, I cannot save the wicked and evil. So truly let the universe and world; people in the universe and beyond including earth know that I will not save anyone that is wicked and evil because they knew and know what they were and are doing.

You don't sacrifice yourself to death for a place in hell and expect someone of Lovey's good and true order to save you. It cannot happen and must never happen. Thus I've told you Lovey, I do not want any strays following me to get into our good and true world; countries and abode; home. I do not need a repeat of evil ever again. I cannot save death. Death must die with their wicked and evil children; own.

Good can no longer cohabitate and live with the wicked and evil of this world. Good must cohabitate and live with good; the good people and spirits of this world and universe. This is what I strive for and if I am amongst the wicked and evil, I will never attain my aim and goal and you know this Lovey. I know your mountain, so truly echo my truth and true peace from their universally and globally; here on earth.

Michelle and Michelle Jean
October 12, 2015
Edited October 15, 2015

It is unfortunate that our lives are not the same Lovey, unfortunate that you are not true to us; cannot abide with us.

In all I seek; I've found lies all around.

I've found despair
Hatred
Loathing
Fear
Prejudice
Death and Hell

In all I seek, I seek the goodness and truth of life. But in all I found, I found confusion, stumbling blocks; the disparity of blacks based on hue.

In all I seek, I've found nonsense; lies based on historical records of man; physical and spiritual indifference; deceit of both worlds.

Yes there is more, but what can I do to teach truth when lies encompass the earth including man – humanity globally?

The damage has been done Lovey and you are to blame.

If you truly wanted to save humanity, you would not have given liars and thieves access to us; our good up good up land and lands; world.

So tell me, how great and true is your loving us so when you cannot do right by us?

You allow evil to find and capture us all the time.

We are slaves here on earth Lovey because you allow men; vile and wicked men and some women and kids to kill.

What good are the commandments of man when no one honours or respect them?

Are we not the Sodomites and Gommorrahites of old globally?

Do we not do perverse things in thy sight here on earth?

Did we not make Egypt and all your lands of goodness and truth a cesspool of sin and evil; wickedness?

Michelle
September 29, 2015

So tell me Lovey, what good are you to us if you allow us to sin reckless and rude?

What good are you to humanity if you cannot overthrow all that is wicked and evil?

What good is giving you my unconditional love of truth and more if you as God cannot abide by the truth; your own true words?

If you cannot abide by you and your true words; how are we as humans going to or expected to?

This makes no sense but yet it happens.

I see and know
Hear and feel

Just this morning (September 29, 2015) I dreamt about the South Pacific, but I cannot tell you what the dream was all about.

The flood comes yes. It is expected because humans truly do not think about the price we have to pay for our sins.

Billions live for greed
Billions live for hope

Many live to kill
Steal

Cheat
Have fun

Many live for fame and glory

Many live to deceive, hence lies and deception in all that we do.

So as earth divide; separate; crumble for some Lovey, truly do all you can to separate all who are good and true from all facets of evil more than infinitely and indefinitely more than forever ever without end.

Michelle and Michelle Jean
September 29, 2015

I know you truly don't like me on this day Lovey because like I've said time and time again, it's the ones that say they love you that screw up your life and hurt you to the point where you want to kill and or destroy yourself.

They leave you so emotionally insane that it takes more than a lifetime to come back sane.

They are the ones to cheat on you and have children outside of their wedded home; home of cleanliness and truth.

They are the ones that say they love you and sacrifice you to death for wealth and fame, political control and dominance, religious divide and lies.

It's the ones that say they love you that stalk you and abuse you brutally because they respect you not.

It's the ones that say they love you that kill you by any means necessary.

You do the same Lovey. You keep us shackled and chained in homes; lands, that are not home to us. You cannot say I am wrong Lovey because you know how I want and need; crave and yearn to leave the land I am in in goodness and in truth more than universally and unconditionally and you keep me trapped here. You do not hear me, thus you cannot truly love, you can only love so.

Remember the message read, *"FOR GOD SO LOVE US HE IS WORTHY TO BE PRAISED."*

So tell me, if you so love us, why do you trap us, hunt us like dogs and leave us in hell with you?

Can truth lie and trap his or her people?
Can truth hand his or her own people over to death to die?

Can truth live a ill and or unclean life? But yet you leave us in unclean surroundings and dwellings. So truly don't tell me about my home being dirty when you are the one to keep me in a dirty home without true and good help. No, I will not blast you, because it goes to show me that you are truly unfair. You've forgotten the way I bug you about my life and the ills in my life.

You've forgotten that I told you I want out. So now tell me, how can I continue to give my truth and honesty to someone that is not true and honest?

How can anyone do this? Thus you are on the sidelines begging humans for a bone; dem what lef an nuh want.

You are our what lef and nuh want because humanity did not choose and chose you.

You do not listen nor do you truly care. So now that someone else have come along and given humans their hearts desire, why should they leave that for you?

It matters not if they are going to die in the end. BILLIONS KNOW THAT THEY ARE GOING TO DIE, AND STILL THEY CONTINUE ON WITH THEIR DIRTY WAYS INSTEAD OF AMENDING IT. So what does that say for you?

You're a joke to humans; thus humans break all your laws globally. So now tell me, what does that truly say about you when it comes to humans?

Should you not move on from us?

You are forever rejected, so accept your loss and losses and move the hell on. Humans have told you categorically that they do not want or need you, but yet you're still hanging on for a shower of rain when it comes to us and I truly do not know why.

Yes I know you've moved on from billions but have you truly?

Tell me something Lovey. What does it profit you to see your own true people suffer like this?

Why should we be battered and bruised, go insane, battle depression and clinical depression because you are not God enough to truly help?

Tell me something, who have you led to your good and true home?

Is that home not closed off to us all day and year long?

We can't even find your home in any given month or year, so why should we stay and cling to someone we truly cannot find; know nothing about?

Yes you are there but you know what, what do we truly need you for if you are not truly there for us?

Not even the earth and environments of earth you can do right and true by. So why you and not someone else?

But I should not talk because humans globally did choose someone else. They did choose a dead man called Jesus as their god, so nothing surprises me when it comes to you in this sense.

You did give us WILL; the right to choose good or evil and humans globally have chosen the latter; evil over good. So blame not humans for your downfall; blame yourself because you knew the outcome of this. You knew humans would choose evil over good.

Truth is something that can never fade Lovey.
Truth builds in a good and positive way.

No, my true love of you will never stray hence I like; truly love the relationship we have in this way.

So I am hoping that you are truly thinking and doing for you and me not in love but in true and more than unconditional love of truth and true peace.

The earth needs true peace and balance Lovey and she cannot get this if wicked and evil people resides in her.

She cannot have this if evil controls the realms of earth and the universe. So truly stop loving so and truly love true.

Like I said, billions did not choose you and you have to let them go because the "WAGES OF SIN IS DEATH," and we all know this but choose to ignore this important fact. We do all manner of evil to self and others and think it's okay when it's truly not okay.

We cannot destroy the home we live in and expect our children to come and fix the mess we created; made. Some messes cannot be fixed and we all know this.

When we disobey you, you leave from us and no matter how we try to get to you, we will never find you. I know this for a fact because you've shown me and told me if I leave you, I will not be able to find you. But in you telling me this Lovey, you too have to do better to secure your good and true people. You have to begin to talk to them soon. And yes, you have to come live with us once again.

See Lovey, true love do not like wars nor do true love seek to kill and destroy and you truly know this. So God up in truth and truly live; abide by all that is truly good and true.

You cannot continue to allow humans to destroy it all. Yes you can say I do not respect you and if you did, you know I will blast you. We are true in all that we do. This is us; we work with each other in truth my way.

So in all that you do Lovey, truly think of you and Mother Earth because in truth see is hurting too.

Michelle
October 12 and 15, 2015

Lovey how can I sow seeds of life; good and true life with you when I doubt and question you?

How can I be your good child when all is changing with me and my sexuality is running wild?

Can I live with someone?
Can I abide with anyone for long?

My spirit desires solitude.

It craves and yearns nature; being one with you and nature.

It craves and yearns the waterways; the purity and clarity of water.

So can I truly live with someone Lovey?

Can I when I want to run away from it all to walk naked and free in the bushes without the peeping toms behind me.

What is freedom to you Lovey?
What is true and good life to you?

Why do I not have an all access pass to you on days like these?

Why am I confused?

No, today I am not lonely and the loneliness is not as often as they use to be. I'm craving nature and the goodness of nature.

I need to be free.
I need to open up to our true and good mystic ways.

I need our true mysticism.

I need to be able to leave my body at will to connect to you.

I need to walk clean and upright to you but you won't let me, why?

Well I know why. Hence one day I truly hope you will solve my battle of will; sexual confusion so that I can truly be free to live good and clean; truly good and clean with you.

Michelle and Michelle Jean
September 29, 2015

I cannot cross this bridge alone
I cannot do it all by myself Lovey
I need you but it seems you don't need me

I crave and yearn your waters of life. All the goodness and truth nature can give me with you.

I long to bathe in your river of crystal clear waters.
Long to connect with you in our own special way.

Oh Lovey if only I can communicate truthfully and wholeheartedly to your female side.

If only she could cherish me as I cherish; more than cherish you?

Mothers know Lovey
Mothers know

So on this day (September 29, 2015) bless me mother with all your goodness and truth so that I may walk prosperously, gloriously; positive and pure in all I do for you and me and our good and true people.

Mama take my hand on this day, never let it go and guide me to you in a good, true, clean and pure way.

Never let me go.
Always truly love me.

As I pray to you on this day for me; let my enemies both great and small; physical and spiritual indefinitely scatter. Let them never rise again or rise up against me.

As you are my beloved and truth, let me be your beloved and truth also.

Continue to protect me.

You are my Mother and Father; I truly thank you for all including our good and true friendship of truth and true love.

Please send the right help that is good and true to help me always because you know I need taking care of. My health and sexuality is not right; they need fixing.

Michelle
September 29, 2015

Lovey is this the calm before the storm?

Dear God I cannot tell. The waters are too calm.

What is happening in the South Pacific?

What is this calm I am seeing in regards to the waterways of life?

Is Oceania going to fully sink?

If so, when Lovey because I truly do not know?

As for the Black Race; Zion fell and the Mongoloid and or Chinese Race is poised to take over.

What's going to happen to Black People on a whole based on deeds and hue? I went there Lovey and I am truly sorry.

We as a people keep rejecting you. We say we want the truth and when the truth comes we destroy it and run to you.

Why destroy the truth?
You never wanted truth in the first place?

I truly don't know on this day Lovey.

We say we want you but keep rejecting you.

We've sold you and self out. Now the Mongolian and or Chinese and or Asian Empire is poised to rule again.

Zion fell Lovey.

Her time has and have expired and woe be unto black people globally.

Babylonians are excluded because they are truly white and not black. Nor do they fall under the black banner of Life.

Michelle and Michelle Jean
September 30, 2015

Oh Lovey October has been nothing but disappointment and drama for me.

Wow because I truly need to move far from family literally.

I need the peace and quiet.

You know what Lovey, my niece and her sister need a reality television show on TLC. Trust me there would be no shortage of drama there.

Tell me something Lovey, why is there bad blood when it comes to siblings that are half sisters and half brothers?

It is beyond me why there is so much rift; family rift.

What is the point of having children if they are going to hate and despise each other?

Not in another lifetime Lovey if there are other lifetimes to be had. Truly not in another lifetime with me and children. Trust me Lovey, if I was to have children in another lifetime I would not have any. It's too hard to raise them by yourself as a mother due to the abandonment of many fathers and mothers.

Life is not valued here on earth so why bring children into a valueless environment or society?

Michelle and Michelle Jean
October 12, 2015

Wow because the dream world is vague now. Some dreams I can remember and some I truly can't whilst others are truly vague.

Fam, I am so not going to bust my brain with this dream because I truly cannot decipher it.

Dreamt a major disaster but I did not see the major disaster so I cannot tell you exactly where the disaster is and or the area this disaster was in.

In the dream I went to this company to say hi to someone. The receptionist knew me. It's like the company was empty and she told me about the disaster that hit. The parent company for the company I was in was in the area that was hit. I cannot remember if she told me the company was hit but I know she told me it was beside a major bank. After she told me that she told me about her mom and how her mother made floral arrangements. She showed me pictures of the different floral arrangements. Some were in white, I believe some were in off pink and some were definitely in red. I ended up getting a small bouquet of red roses that was in a square or rectangular clear casing that looked like a box but it wasn't a box. In the dream, when you see or saw the picture of the flowers; you were actually getting them in your hand if my English makes any sense. I also saw a picture of her mother and she was not old but young. Do not quote me on the colour of her mother's dress but I think it was light blue. At the end she gave me her mother's card and some other cards. Oh man I cannot decipher this but I have to wait and see if there is a death in my family. We are long overdue. Don't say it or go there people because we know when someone is going to die in our family. The flowers is just the beginning stage. Anyway after all that happened this tall and handsome white man that was in a grey suit took me to lunch. He was the owner I believe but for sure he was a top executive in the company. Also in the dream it seemed like we were dating under the quiet. We went for a walk but everywhere we went for lunch was closed. We back tracked and walked to this school; university. But when we tried to go into a particular section of the school the water came rushing up angrily and crashed into the bridge and or the area you would walk to get into the school. So we could not go into the school to have lunch. We had to leave so we back tracked again. Whilst walking you could see the eerie feeling around us because the other buildings or lecture halls were abandoned leaving an eerie feeling. We continued to walk and talk. I was telling him about my PS3 that my son broke. I asked him about his family and if he wanted children and he said yes but in five (5) years. In the dream I said to myself I won't be able to give you any. He was younger than me people and I am up there in age, thus my baby bearing days are over. I asked him about his family and he told me about his brother and sister. Suffice it to say we did not have lunch and he walked me to the subway where we hugged and bid each other adieu. He was a perfect gentleman because he stayed with me and made sure I got on the subway okay. Walking towards the subway I looked back and he waved at me and I waved at him until I was out of sight. The subway was odd too because it looked nothing like a Canadian Subway to me. There was so many seats that people could sit on whist waiting for the train. The seats were blue and not that pleasing in my eye to sit on but I managed to find a seat and I woke up out of my sleep.

As for the season I believe it was autumn to winter but no snow was on the ground.

So Fam, I truly don't know about this dream like I said. The school could be UFT (University of Toronto) but I cannot tell you for sure because this university is not situated beside the lake. The only school I know of is George Brown College. I will not read anything into this dream because I truly don't know. I don't know if disaster is going to hit downtown Toronto but something is going to happen somewhere. I just have to watch and see. Like I said, I did not see the destruction of Toronto but something is going to happen if anything happens at all. I cannot tell you if this is a dream in a dream because I truly do not know. I saw the water raging, so no one could cross the bridge to get into the school but the actual disaster I did not see.

Have I had similar dreams like this in content?

Yes.

I also dreamt these two dogs. Man were they trouble to me. There was a big dog and a small dog and they both

had black and white coating and or colour. People and Fam, di dawg dem run wey. Could I catch dem?
Wow.

I chased after them and one ran up in a tree. I can't remember if it's because the bigger dog saw a squirrel ran up in the tree, but di dawg ran up in the tree and I said to myself in the dream dawg can climb tree?

The little dawg seeing the big dawg run up inna di tree ran up in the tree.

Di big dwag jump out and di likkle dawg jump outta eee tree an tek off. People and Fam, when di likkle dawg jump outta eee tree mi tink sey im dead; a guh bruk up but di dawg tek off. An me like ediat a run dem dung. When I did catch up I noticed that they; both dogs had scaring on them.

Did I catch them?

No because they took off again saying they are going to go to the United States. I eventually caught one of them, the dogs and ended up with poop in my hand. The dog was crapping and ended getting it's feces on my hand for which I wiped on the ground but did not get all of the crap off my hand. Thus I know what this dream is all about, and Lovey I ask that you keep me out of sibling rivalry when it comes to my niece and her sister. I truly do not want or need to get into this mix up because the dream prior to this with the poop and dogs at my niece's home has come to head. The feuding has and have started and it's not pretty. I truly do not want or need the mix up right now in my life. October has been a month so far that is filled with utter disappointment for me.

I know the scars are there between sisters and they will never heal because both sisters are carrying them.

It's sad that in our lives that family have to fight against family due to the bullshit of he said she said or she said he said or he said she said.

Dysfunctional wow; thus I've told you Lovey in some of my other books that every child deserves a mother and a father. It is wrong in my book but not in yours to have children for this man and that man. The rivalry is there and it is sad that some families cannot get over this rivalry. I have it in my own family and it's truly a shame when children of same mother but different father or same father and different mother pit and or put strife amongst each other.

I cannot say if this hatred you are born with. No, some of the traits are learned due to what they see. Thus life is a bitch when you have half anything.

Michelle and Michelle Jean
October 13, 2015

Lovey, I talk the talk; now I have to walk our good and true walk.

Why did we let you go Lovey?
Why can we not see the truth?

When you take away our right and rights to life; what do we as a people have left?

When you take our identity from us; what do we have left?

When you take our culture from us; what do we have left?

As blacks globally we are left with nothing. Many have tried and failed with us because we do not want to break free of our conditioned state of mind.

We do not want to break free of our weakened state and state of mind.

Like Bob Marley said, "what we know is what they tell us," but I know differently.

When are we as a race of people going to wake up and stand up and say no more?

We as black people (not based on hue) have such a rich and lush history; culture, but yet we give it up to become a part of the collective of sin; wickedness and evil. Why Lovey, why?

Can we not see our own destruction; destructive path?

As a race and nation, we say we need the truth but from what I see, we do not.

We talk but do little for our own people.

We say we are concerned but we are not.

We are no longer the beacon of life because we are filled with apathy. Hence we disassociate self from you Lovey and worship false god and gods including man.

Michelle
September 30, 2015

Where is my way out Lovey?
Where is my way out?

A storm is coming but when it hits I truly don't know.

My life is filled with woes; hate.

There is too much anger and pain in my children.
Too much self hate. No, not self hate but anger towards each other.

The sibling rivalry is insane and I truly cannot take it, hence I block it out. Thus it is wise for a woman to only have children for one man and one man only.

Lovey, there is this much hatred when it comes to sibling rivalry?

Why?

Is it only my family that you find this sibling rivalry; hatred?

The fuss is there but I truly cannot deal with it. Hence I truly want to cut; go and live on my own. My children are of age and I cannot take the bullshit of family feuds; hatred. I despise this in humans, thus peace; true peace is rare in our surroundings including household. I've put up with enough and I am done. This is also why I tell you I am going home. I cannot take the infighting of my children nor can I take the stress of them.

I cannot deal with the lies; hence I have to truly find my own way and leave them.

Michelle
September 30, 2015

Lovey, are my storms and battles over?
Am I on my way to true peace and freedom with you?

Lovey, why did we as black people not get it?
Why did we fall like this?
Why did Zion have to go back to Asia?

Well I know black people resided in Asia and Asia is black land but why let Africa fail you; continue to fail you?

We say we are of Nuba; Nubian but what does Nubian mean? Not by man's standard but by yours.

Isn't Nubia a planet?

Isn't that where true evil; possession comes from?

Is this not the planet of black demons?

Lovey, am I grasping at straws?

Are we as black people the true black people or are we the fake ones; the true demonic broods?

Does evil not dwell upon us as a race and nation of people?

Did our forefathers not sacrifice us to death so that they could be a part of the devil's perverse and unclean world?

Did Egypt not become perverse?

Was Egypt not filled with every manner of sexual perversion on the face of this planet?

Did our people not become Abdullah's; servants and slaves to Death's children and people?

Did these people not crucify us; whip us into accepting their defiled and nasty languages and customs thus defiling you Lovey?

So tell me, where do we truly belong with you in all of this; when as a nation of people; we continually reject you?

Hell is full of black people Lovey, so what say you?
What say you Lovey?

Michelle and Michelle Jean
October 01, 2015

Lovey, how can we be free in this world when there is so much pitting going on?

How can we be free when this race hates the next?

Let me ask you something, does evil not disguise themself as you?

At times does evil not come to me pretending to be you?

I see this and know this and I lash out at you. You are the only one I can lash out at because you constantly let evil reach me.

I know I have spiritual and physical enemies; more spiritual than physical because I do not associate out of my comfort zone; nor do I want and need a lot of people around me.

Friends and family I can do without in truth; hence truth and true love is hard to find here on earth.

I truly do not need or want friends and family. I need true friends and a true family. When we have truth we have all. Thus I strive for and life for goodness and truth including honesty and cleanliness.

Yes I know I will create a lot of enemies here on earth but that matters to me. *I know EVIL DOES NOT LIKE ANYONE THAT IS GOOD AND TRUE. IN ALL THAT EVIL DOES AND DO; EVIL TRIES AND DO ALL TO ELIMINATE ALL WHO ARE*

<u>GOOD AND TRUE.</u> *Evil cannot live with good, thus evil kill good and take everything for self; as their own.*

Therefore, I have to wonder about you sometimes Lovey. All this you see and know but yet help us not. No, I should not say that. You are an excellent protector but a lousy teacher and father; giver.

Yes you've shown me all that would happen to me before they happen thus I know my end. We all do if we are true messengers and messengers of you.

Did Martin Luther King Jr. not tell his people he was going to die with his I have a dream speech.

Did Bob Marley not tell his people he was going to die in Chances Are?

Have I not told them of my death?

Have I not told you, I do not want to die in this country and you are not listening to me?

So we know our end, it's a matter of when it comes and how soon it comes. Thus the life of the flesh here on earth for good people is truly limited.

<u>Evil people do wrong and live long, but good cannot do wrong and live long period.</u> Why couldn't it be the other way around Lovey?

Good live long; forever ever all around and evil die young; right away.

Ah Lovey this is me on this day because the body it truly weak and not well.

I need to sleep but I cannot.

The weather has and have changed and it's back to limited sleep for me. I need something different but what?

House is truly not peaceful at nights anymore. Too much dead walking about and I cannot sleep half naked anymore. I have to cover up because I truly do not want the dead interfering with me in that way.

Sum bole face eee noa.
Dem nuh cya.

Thus I better leave this topic alone because I know the dead; some dead sleep with people in the living.

Michelle and Michelle Jean
October 13, 2015

Lovey like you I am tired of my Black own not knowing the truth and adhering to the truth.

So tell me now Lovey, what say you on Islam?

Have the devil and his nasty and condemned own not polluted it and introduced their filth and language to it?

Did you not forbid your people (the true Jews) to stay the hell away from it?

So why is Africa littered with it; Islam?

But then again Lovey I should not come to you with this because I am disgracing you and I am truly sorry. You know my truth thus I feel sorry for no black man or woman that joins this faith as of this day and become slaves.

Wi too fool fool.

Jah noa, well you Lovey noa.

Wi fool fool eeee.

When are we going to learn that Islam is condemned and it is death of mind body and spirit?

Look at the globe Lovey and see how wretched the people have and has become because of them.

Look at Russia and the influence of Babylon in their structure.

No Lovey truly look at that land and tell me why.

Why Babylon has a root and history there?

Yes I know the truth and the tag along due to Moses from Africa into China.

As for me Lovey, I want and need none (Babylonians) in our kingdom and kingdoms, land and lands; home and new home. None can tag along with us because they are rejected more than unconditionally and more than infinitely and indefinitely. I don't care if some are of mixed race and lineage; none is welcomed because I've made none and or any of them apart of our good and true foundation (s) and frameworks of truth and goodness; life.

Michelle and Michelle Jean
October 01, 2015

I will not feel sorry for my own black people when all is said and done Lovey.

They want to suffer with death in hell truly let them.

You have tried time and time again with us and we are the ones to reject and fail you.

We are the ones to continue to turn against you.

We are the ones to accept death and other people's language and culture and say it's ours.

We gave up our rights and customs Lovey.

We have nothing because we were not proud and satisfied with what we have and or had.

The nastiness suited us fine.

Go back to Solomon of the bible.

Did he not fail you?

All you told him not to do he did?

Am I not failing you also? I want to go back to my homeland. Not because of hate or spite but because there is where I can afford. Yes things are in a poor state down there and I will go back with nothing.

People will look down on me but I truly don't care. Yes you've shown me my life – death there, but I've told you, I am willing to take that chance because I am truly not happy here in the North.

I am a prisoner here mentally, spiritually and financially.

I am broken all around. I've pleaded with you for good and true life including financial stability and you do not hear me.

I've pleaded with you for stability, truth with us and for us and still you do not hear me.

I've pleaded with you for my health and strength and still you do not hear me.

I've pleaded with you and to you for goodness and truth for the good and true seeds you've given me and still you do not hear me. So what am I to do?

I cannot stay in your jail with you so I have to go and find true life on my own.

Michelle Jean
October 01, 2015

Oh Lovey is October one of those months that's going to bring me nothing but disappointment financially, mentally and spiritually?

Lovey what's going on in my household?

Lovey am I miserly?

No I am not but yet I find 3 of my children are miserly when it comes to money.

The fourth one is iffy but he's not miserly when it comes to me financially.

What he give me I have to hold on to it because money doesn't stay in his hand. So what he gives me I usually spend it back on him.

I don't know Lovey.

Do I truly want to divorce my children; all of them?

Yes I do.

Maybe it's me.

No it's not me. I give truthfully but with them there are certain character traits I truly do not like with them and in them.

Yes they can say the same about me because my emotions is like a roller coaster sometimes.

I don't treat any different I don't think but they would say otherwise.

I give all fair treatment but yet the older two say otherwise when it comes to the last two.

Do I treat my last two better than the first?

Do I not try to treat all equally in terms of my truth; giving despite the disrespect I get all around.

Thus Lovey, please tell me and show me my unfairness in life and in my household so that I can correct them and make my life thoroughly clean; whole?

Michelle and Michelle Jean
October 02, 2015

FREEDOM

I am but a dream
Hope
I am like a desert
Dry but at times moist

I am land
I am sea
The rivers that flows; meet

I am woman
I am free
I am me

Michelle Jean

What do we perceive life to be Lovey?

What is life; true life in truth?
What is free to some?

Are our lives not different?
Changing

For some money is of no worth; whereas for others they cannot live without it.

So with all this said, what is true life to you Lovey?

Is it a barren land void of warmth and truth?

Is it a land that has not been impacted by negative climate change; the pollutants humans emit in the atmosphere, stratosphere; the ground ground beneath the earth?

Is your true land filled with trees and water; good food to eat; sacred and or pure waters to drink and bathe in?

Can all this be found again here on earth?

Has the greed of man – humans not destroyed earth and you?

Do humans not value money over life?
Do we humans not destroy and kill for money?

So how can we value you Lovey when money is the game; the game and play of humans?

Life is not sacred anymore.

Nature is not valued anymore.

Spirituality of self; mind body and spirit is nonexistent.

Our spirituality has and have been replace by the church; the greed of man that sell God; you and other gods for prophet, sorry profit.

No don't look at me because what I put away for you and our people including waterways is for them. A good home in a land where I will be happy and free I need. But the confines of man's political and religious systems I truly do not need.

Michelle and Michelle Jean
October 04, 2015

What is life without freedom Lovey?
What is life if we are shackled and chained?

What is life if we are not secluded and segregated from the hustle and bustle of society?

What man call freedom is truly not freedom.
What man call life is truly not life.

From humans are governed by political lies and secular lies; jokes; deceit, then we are not free.

Religion traps and kills the spirit.
Political forces and or politics keeps us shackled and chained, shackled and chained to the system they've created. A system where it's impossible to break free to truly live on your own.

You are not free to think.
You are not free to travel to different lands; countries.

In all that humans; we as humans do; we limit each other, kill each other, tell lies on each other.

So in all that we as humans do, we do not live to live; we live to die.

Yes we are to blame for this because we give others control over our lives; hence the governance of man; man to man is unjust and truly unclean; dirty.

Mans soul is no longer pure; thus the outer and inner is truly dirty; polluted all around.

Michelle and Michelle Jean
October 04, 2015

Can a man live in a free society again Lovey?

Can a man truly be free without the lust of money; bit coins?

Can we truly go back to living on the land and respecting the land without man and violence; bloodshed?

Can wrongs justify rights?
Can rights justify wrongs?

A good society is free. It cannot be controlled.
It is self sufficient, self reliant, honest and true; good and pure.

Good societies share within; take care of its own before they take care of others.

Good societies are not dependant on others for anything because they have all they need.

Good societies do not kill. They preserve and take care of their true and precious own.

No one can go hungry in a good society because we truly take care of our own.

Good societies do not seek to create strife with others.

Good societies crave and yearn peace in all that they do.

They respect nature; are true and good to nature.

They keep the air, trees, land and waterways clean all the time.

Good societies shy away from and run away from all that is wicked and evil.

Good societies do all they can to separate and not integrate with the wicked and evil of this world.

Good societies know not evil because they are good and true.

Michelle and Michelle Jean
October 04, 2015

Lovey wicked and evil societies kill; conquer and kill.

Rob and or steal.

Dominate and control.

Subdue and keep their people and the conquered poor; abused and shamed; shackled and chained; enslaved.

So Lovey who and what are you?

Are you not a part of the masculine forces and or gender in the spiritual world and or realm that keep humanity captive; controlled?

Yes I know you are female, more female than male; so why do we say HIM?

Yes I know the XY and not XX thus 3XY.

No, I won't go there because I know the definite and indefinite truth of you and yes me and our good and true people.

But Lovey, what about freedom?

As humans we tear down nature to build all that our heart desires without thought of our true future.

Some abandon areas and leave these burnt out and dilapidated buildings in place. Instead of building new, rebuild, restore in the areas that have been abandoned, we build and destroy other areas only to abandon them and start the destructive process all over again.

So what is freedom Lovey when Earth herself is not free from the destructive nature of humans?

Michelle and Michelle Jean
October 04, 2015

It's amazing how we say we are free when in truth we are not. We are being manipulated and controlled in thought, religion, social media and media (advertising and news), politics, sex, marital (homosexual and heterosexual affairs) and or family affairs.

"Mom I did not know homosexuality was a sin. I didn't know it's in the bible." This my last child said to me and I said, did man not write the bible. How does a man know what God says? I also told him homosexuality is not wrong.

Do not throw your hands up in the air and fume because not one of you knows what Lovey wants. Hence, <u>**WE LET OTHER HUMAN BEINGS TAKE OUR RIGHT AND RIGHTS TO LIFE FROM US.**</u>

Yes Lovey can tell you who to love and or be with, but to tell another human being that homosexuality is wrong is a grave injustice.

THIS WORLD IS NOT BASED ON THE HETEROSEXUAL GENDER ALONE. <u>**Homosexuals are there and you cannot discriminate against a person for their sexual preference.**</u> **IT IS** <u>**UNIVERSALLY AND GLOBALLY; ETHICALLY AND MORALLY WRONG.**</u>

And no, I will not stick up for anyone that is transgender BECAUSE THEY ARE MORALLY AND ETHICALLY WRONG.

THEY ARE A SIN AND CONDEMNATION TO EVERY HUMAN BEING ON THE FACE OF THIS PLANET. THEY ARE ALSO A SIN AND CONDEMNATION TO EVERY GOOD AND EVIL SPIRIT IN THE SPIRITUAL REALM.

You cannot change your gender from male to female and change your birth certificate to say you are a female when you were born a male and still a male despite the hormones you are taking.

You cannot change your gender from female to male and change your birth certificate to say you are a male when you were born a female and still a female despite the hormones you are taking.

You are wrong thus you've condemned your family; all your family to a lifetime of servitude in hell. ***Your contamination IS YOUR CONDEMNATION THUS YOUR HELL IN HELL.***

Yes death has to take your wretched souls but it's not the regular death that takes you, thus the different death's that take humanities spirit from the living.

Thus I truly good luck to the doctors, nurses, hospitals, countries and or lands, judges, clergy that grant you access to the legal and judicial systems of earth; perform your operations and give you rights to change. Woe, truly woe be unto them because their hell will be grave.

Wow because not one of them including family will be saved. You do not justify lies by saying a lie is right and this is what you people have done.

You justify lies by falsifying the records and life of these people thus you sinned big time.

You also took away the life; the right of your family members to live. Know this, if their name was in the book of life, Lovey have to transfer their name into the book of death because of what you have done. You condemned them and there is no remittance of sin for condemnation and you know this. Well if you don't you know now.

YOU CANNOT CHANGE THE RECORD BOOKS OF MAN TO SUIT THIS TYPE OF CONDEMNATION. And no, you cannot get around it by saying these people were hermaphrodites because they were not born hermaphrodites. When a hermaphrodite can choose their sex, these people cannot because they were born either a true male and or a true female.

"TRUTH IS EVERLASTING LIFE"

So when you change the truth and live by your lies you cannot have everlasting life. You are condemning yourself in the living. And I've told you time and time again, *"the life you live in the living determines were you go in death* _and or after your spirit sheds the flesh."_ So truly know what you are doing.

Like I've said, **_it's the ones that say they love you that take away your life. They screw you up so badly that you are left more than broken and insane._**

If we truly loved; you would not take away from the life of you, nor would you take away from the good life of this earth and universe including other humans.

I've told you, if the devil could not get into Lovey's kingdom and or abode he was not going to let you get in. He was going to do all to keep you from Lovey and Lovey from you and he's succeed in doing this.

Thus humans are truly not free because we shed the flesh to go to hell and die.

AND NO THERE IS NO LIFE IN DEATH, JUST TRUE PAIN. THUS HELL; THE HELL BILLIONS OF HUMANS MUST NOW FACE IN THE SPIRIT BEFORE YOUR SPIRIT DIES.

And no, Jesus cannot say he died to save humanity because not all of humanity and or all the people in humanity; this *earth belongs to Lovey. Good has their own race of people and bad (the devil for some) has their own race of people. So one man cannot save all because like I said, we are not all of and from Lovey.*

Furthermore, one man cannot save the world because Lovey ordained no one to save all of humanity. You all know this.

Jesus had 12 disciples and they preached.

This just tells me Jesus is one half of death. He commanded half the globe and or the people in the world to follow him thus the Christian kingdom, and Mohammad commanded the other half which is the Islamic kingdom. Thus the two portions of death. Physical and spiritual death. One in the living and the other being final death in the spiritual realm.

So in all that we do, we are truly not free because we live in confined societies that tell us what to wear, who to marry, how look, what to eat, when and how to have sex, where to live, what to drink, how to worship, how to dance, how to talk and walk, how to sleep plus a whole lot more.

So now tell me, what is freedom, true freedom to you?

What is your life worth to you?
Do you value your life?

No you don't because you are not free. Freedom isn't war and strike.

Freedom does not misguide spiritually or religiously including politically.

Freedom is not being bound or being told you cannot travel to this or that land freely because not one human own a part or parcel of land on this earth. I know the land papers that were given to me, but you know what let me leave this alone because it's not every land on the face of this planet I want to go into. Some lands are forbidden to me and rightfully. So because humans have and has made certain lands that we live in, the dung of the earth literally.

Stop, because the land and lands some of you live in were stolen by your ancestors from the original inhabitants of the earth; so truly don't go there.

NOT ONE HUMAN BEING ON THE FACE OF THIS PLANET HAS THEIR GGLC OR GLC; GOOD GOD LAND CERTIFICATE OR GOD LAND CERTIFICATE. NOT ONE OF YOU CAN PRODUCE THIS CERTIFICATE FROM LOVEY, GOOD GOD AND ALLELUJAH. COME ON NOW. SO WHAT SAY YOU? *Humans are thieves that rape the earth of all then turn around and claim her as theirs; when earth do not belong to any of you. So earth too is not free because she cannot get rid of her cancer sticks and plagues that plague her in a negative way.* **<u>She too is stuck in hell;</u>** *a hell that was created by us humans.*

Don't with your bullshit scrolls because no scroll of man is of Lovey. Men wrote their bullshit to deceive you and say they are of God. Please.

If these scrolls were of Lovey, the true and living God, then humans would not be sinning until this day. Things would have changed for the better because humans would not sin. They would live in true peace and do all in goodness and in truth to keep the peace.

Michelle and Michelle Jean
October 14, 2015
Edited October 15, 2015

I can hear the sound of the wind
I feel its force
Knock me down why don't ya

Let me feel the cool breeze lifting me gently; playing with my skin.

Delicious are you
Wind gritting my teeth
Playing sweet melodies to me

Yes I can hear the sound of the wind

I can feel its strength
The freshness of its breath

Ah the wind

Knock me down
Play with my skin
Cool my body down

Wrap me in your cool embrace and let me thank you again and again.

Michelle and Michelle Jean
October 04, 2015

I want to be naked amongst the trees
Want to know and feel nature all around me

I want to speak to nature
Walk like the natural mystics do

I want and need to create good and true; pure and clean life with nature.

Want the grass under my feet to be forever ever green and pure; void of all insects and creepy crawlers.

No bugs of the unkind nature. Just pure, good, honest and true peace; tranquility.

Healing waters must we have all year round including purity of sand and beach.

Aah yes, I want to be naked in nature. Spending the rest of my life, good and pure life, for more than all eternity in true unison and harmony with nature; the trees, waterways, earth and all that is good and true, honest and pure in nature.

Michelle and Michelle Jean
October 04, 2015

There is no racism in death, so why is there racism in life?

When did we as humans become so unforgiving that we have to kill each other for sport; game?

We're not humans but barbarians that know not the value and gift of life.

We say we care, but yet watch other nations kill, demean and eradicate in the name of science and religion.

So no, we are not human beings, but devils that plague the earth for the sole purpose of destruction and death.

Michelle and Michelle Jean
October 07, 2015

Sometimes I have to wonder what is freedom
What constitutes freedom
Free will
Free spirit and mind

Are we not like caged animals in a flesh that keep us prisoners from the truth?

Are we not prisoners to life and death Lovey?

So what is freedom if we are not truly free?

Are you free to us Lovey?
Are we truly free to reach you?

Are we not lost when it comes to the truth of you?

So what is freedom without truth and true life?

Michelle Jean
October 07, 2015

How can I chase the blues away Lovey?

How can I get rid of the emptiness in me when it comes to you?

Sometimes I ache but today the aching is truly not there.

I just feel trapped by you.
Trapped in a maze that I cannot get out of when it comes to you.

Restrictions are many when it comes to me and you, but I guess this is truly you. But why should I live in a restricted world with you?

Why should I have to die with you and alongside you?

Why can't we live together in true peace and harmony; true unity?

Why can't we grow together positively in unison?

Ah Lovey, I truly don't know on this day.

Michelle
October 07, 2015

The breasts are aching due to the way I sleep.

Ah yes, I truly need my mind to be free and void of the restrictions placed upon me.

Lovey, untie me and let me be free.
Stop hindering me. I am truly fed up of it.

You chose your world and yes I did choose you, but I refuse to live in your limited world.

I refuse to be caged with you when we can truly be free.

Create a good and true world; place with me where we can both be free. Come on now.

I hate my limited space. It's too confined; claustrophobic.

My spirit needs freedom – freedom to travel; roam excessively.

So Lovey, truly free us from the confines of hell.

Michelle
October 07, 2015

Musical Mix

Money Worries	The Maytones
Murderer	Barrington Levy
Lovindeer	Don't Bend Down
Admiral Tibet	Babylon Brutality

Dedicated to all in humanity who truly want true peace and freedom for self and the land or country they live in.

Admiral Tibet	Call Me A Warrior
Admiral Tibet	Serious Times

Beres Hammond   Love From A Distance

Some of us should truly listen to this song and free themselves because in all we do, we need to stop the hate and stop telling people how they should live. ***The right to live and or life is not up to the next person, it's up to you.*** Some wrongs are not forgiven, but it is you who made the choice to live wrong and die. It is you that took the ones you claim to love to hell with you. Thus you had no true love for the ones you claim to love. And truly do not look at me when it comes to wicked and evil people and the transgender society because ***WE ALL KNOW THAT TRUTH IS EVERLASTING LIES NOT LIES.***

Michelle

I should have uploaded this book to Lulu yesterday but totally forgot to do so. Now it's October 16, 2015 and I am in a state of total confusion.

I am truly dazed and confused because I keep dreaming about water and destruction as well as the South Pacific. Why the South Pacific? Hence I have to ask again, if all of Oceanic; the South Pacific going to sink?

Fam and people I truly cannot figure it out because I truly don't know what to do or think. I truly don't know who to go to and say look into this, something is going to happen. All I can do is write and hope that someone can figure out these destructive and or destruction dreams for me and you.

Maybe it's me, turmoil is coming in my life and I will be in danger, but I know something is truly not right; thus the pig's feet I saw this morning.

Dear God what's going on with the Young Black Youths?

What is going to happen to them because pig's feet is truly not good in the spiritual realm.

Black Youths please wake up and start doing right for yourself because the prognosis in the dream world is truly not good for any of you. You have to wake up if you want to be saved. Start looking into your future because I do not *see a good one for any of you and I truly want to cry. I feel it for you because the doors are closing for many of you globally. **So truly LISTEN TO REAL SITUATION BY BOB MARLEY BECAUSE THIS DESTRUCTION IS UNSTOPPABLE.***

*NONE OF US CAN RUN FROM THIS DESTRUCTION. America dear God America!! They are slated to fall and destruction is looming and or on the horizon for this land. I saw it and no one can stop this destruction. America has been ordained to fall; be destroyed. So truly look into yourself and walk away from the wrongs you are doing please. **Please I am begging you to start listening to good council because not even the messengers of Lovey can stop the destructions that are coming on earth.** OUR SINS HAVE GONE BEYOND THE LIMIT, THUS WE MUST BE DESTROYED. Please listen to my plea and do all that is good and true to save yourself. You cannot let death take you to hell to face your hell. Please listen. All that you can amend, start amending them because we are at critical mass. So listen to good and true council. I cannot reach you in the living, but if these words can reach you please let them reach you. Please, please, please save yourself.*

Am I scared right now?

Yes and the tears are coming because all I see is destruction and I cannot tell you where; which land is going to be devastated and or destroyed. Maybe it's crazy me but I truly don't think so.

This morning I dreamt I was in this business place; factory and the owner told me he's changing out the electrical sockets of the building and or company. He was complaining that the landlord refuses to change them. They needed changing because they were short circuiting. Fam and people I do not know this white man that was of skinny to medium built. He's medium height to tall and was in dark clothing. I think he had black hair and he was say in his mid forties to fifties. I can't remember if he had a red shirt and black plants on but he was wearing dark clothing.

No he was not bad looking either.

In the dream he began to do repairs on the electrical circuits. I was at this desk and I believe this portly white gentleman with black hair in a grey suit came by my desk and said something to me then left. I truly did not see his face because his head was bowed low. When he left I looked at the electrical socket beside me. You could see the wires sticking out and the socket began to spark but fire did not come out, this white substance came out. Think snow people and you will get the idea of the white substance that was coming out of the socket. I believe the owner of the business said, "you see." Leaving the building I went outside and I saw a highway and this truck; trailer truck crossed the highway. The highway was high up people. I don't know if highway bridge is the best word to use but it was a highway with a high overpass. When the trailer truck and tractor trailer truck passed the section I stood, the highway collapsed in the water. People ended up in the water and the highway came down on them. Some swam to shore but I did not see anyone dead and or any death. When I saw the people swimming to shore I said, "what about the South Pacific," and or something to that effect but I know I said something about the South Pacific. So I truly don't know. Maybe it's my chaotic world and it's me that's going to be under fire for what is written in some of these books. Oh I forgot. Before the portly white man came to my desk, this white nurse came to my desk and took my book and the reading on her meter said, 7.9... She had other numbers written down and she said the numbers were good. The blood part came through this morning because someone did take my blood.

I cannot decipher this dream and I will not decipher it because I can't. I cannot tell you if a part of highway 401 in Toronto is going to collapse because I truly do not know where any of this highway pass over water.

So for the countries that have highways going over water truly be careful because destruction cometh.

It's the same for the university beside the sea. All countries that have universities beside and or near seas or oceans truly be on guard and be careful. As for time line, I truly cannot give you this because the timeline of death has and have changed for me. Plus I am so not keeping tabs on my destruction dreams anymore.

Yes it could be Toronto that is hit by these destructions but I am not sure. These places are not familiar to me here in Canada and I've told you time and time again death masks death for me.

Maybe I have to change my course and go to Guam and or somewhere in the South Pacific and see for myself.

Fam and people I truly don't know. For me to see destruction two nights in a row is truly new for and to me. Maybe this is my new beginning here on earth who knows. Yes I am grasping at straws but if you are into dreams and know how to decipher them; please DM me at MichelleJean77 on twitter.

Michelle

OTHER BOOKS BY MICHELLE JEAN

Blackman Redemption – The Fall of Michelle Jean
Blackman Redemption – After the Fall Apology
Blackman Redemption – World Cry – Christine Lewis
Blackman Redemption
Blackman Redemption – The Rise and Fall of Jamaica
Blackman Redemption – The War of Israel
Blackman Redemption – The Way I Speak to God
Blackman Redemption – A Little Talk With Man
Blackman Redemption – The Den of Thieves
Blackman Redemption – The Death of Jamaica
Blackman Redemption – Happy Mother's Day
Blackman Redemption – The Death of Faith
Blackman Redemption – The War of Religion
Blackman Redemption – The Death of Russia
Blackman Redemption – The Truth
Blackman Redemption – Spiritual War
Blackman Redemption – The Youths
Blackman Redemption – Black Man Where Is Your God?

The New Book of Life
The New Book of Life – A Cry For The Children
The New Book of Life – Judgement
The New Book of Life – Love Bound
The New Book of Life – Me
The New Book of Life – Life

Just One of Those Days
Book Two – Just One of Those Days
Just One of Those Days – Book Three The Way I Feel
Just One of Those Days – Book Four

The Days I Am Weak
Crazy Thoughts – My Book of Sin
Broken
Ode to Mr. Dean Fraser

A Little Little Talk
A Little Little Talk – Book Two

Prayers
My Collective
A Little Talk/A Time For Fun and Play
Simple Poems
Behind The Scars
Songs of Praise And Love

Love Bound
Love Bound – Book Two

Dedication Unto My Kids
More Talk
Saving America From A Woman's Perspective
My Collective the Other Side of Me
My Collective the Dark Side of Me
A Blessed Day
Lose To Win
My Doubtful Days – Book One

My Little Talk With God
My Little Talk With God – Book Two

A Different Mood and World – Thinking

My Nagging Day
My Nagging Day – Book Two

Friday September 13, 2013
My True Love
It Would Be You
My Day

A Little Advice – Talk
1313, 2032, 2132 – The End of Man
Tata

MICHELLE'S BOOK BLOG – BOOKS 1 – 22

My Problem Day
A Better Way
Stay – Adultery and the Weight of Sin – Cleanliness
Message

Let's Talk
Lonely Days – Foundation
A Little Talk With Jamaica – As Long As I Live
Instructions For Death
My Lonely Thoughts
My Lonely Thoughts – Book Two
My Morning Talks – Prayers With God
What A Mess
My Little Book
A Little Word With You
My First Trip of 2015
Black Mother – Mama Africa
Islamic Thought
My California Trip January 2015
My True Devotion by Michelle – Michelle Jean
My Many Questions To God
My Talk
My Talk Book Two

My Talk Book Three – The Rise of Michelle Jean
My Talk Book Four
My Talk Book Five
My Talk Book Six
My Talk Book Seven
My Talk Book Eight – My Depression
My Talk Book Nine – Death
My Talk Book Ten – Wow
My Day – Book Two
My Talk Book Eleven – What About December?
Haven Hill
What About December – Book Two
My Talk Book Twelve – Summary and or Confusion
My Talk Book Thirteen
My Talk Book Fourteen – My Talk With God
My Talk Book Fifteen – My Talk